THE KYBALION

THE KYBALION

by Three Initiates

The Masterwork of Esoteric Wisdom
For Living with Power and Purpose

Abridged and Introduced
by Mitch Horowitz

THE CONDENSED CLASSICS LIBRARY™

Published by Gildan Media LLC
aka G&D Media.
www.GandDmedia.com

The Kybalion was originally published in 1908
G&D Media Condensed Classics edition published 2018
Abridgement and Introduction copyright © 2017 by Mitch
Horowitz

FIRST EDITION: 2018

Cover design by David Rheinhardt of Pyrographx

Interior design by Meghan Day Healey of Story Horse, LLC.

ISBN: 978-1-7225-0046-7

To Hermes Trismegistus
known by the ancient Egyptians as
"The Great Great"
and "Master of Masters"
this little volume of Hermetic teachings
is reverently dedicated

Contents

Why *The Kybalion* Matters

The short book called *The Kybalion*, published in 1908, is probably the most popular and, in my estimation, most important occult work of the twentieth century.

The book is rivaled in significance only by a much longer and very different work, Manly P. Hall's magisterial encyclopedia arcana, *The Secret Teachings of All Ages*, which appeared twenty years later. The landscape of mythical and esoteric philosophies that the scholar Hall curated, illustrated, and documented in his volume are, in a sense, distilled into their practical philosophical essentials in the precise guidebook *The Kybalion*, written under the pseudonymous byline of Three Initiates.

As I've written elsewhere, and will not cover in any great detail here, Three Initiates was one of several pseudonyms used by Chicago publisher, lawyer, and

New Thought philosopher, William Walker Atkinson, whom historical and documentary sources have identified as the book's sole author. Atkinson was also its publisher at his Yogi Publication Society, a longtime and widely loved occult press. But unveiling the mystery of the book's authorship in no way detracts from its scope and achievement.

The greatness of *The Kybalion* is that Atkinson successfully captures—and makes relevant for modern seekers—elements of the late-ancient Greek-Egyptian philosophy called Hermeticism. Hermeticism grew out of the intellectual ferment of the city of Alexandria in the decades immediately following Christ. In the closing generations of Egyptian antiquity, a diffuse collection of Greek writers—who were part of the Hellenic ruling class that presided over the fading empire—encountered the priesthoods, temple orders, and initiatory religions of Egypt's dissipating spiritual culture. Using Greek literary form, these scribes produced a variety of dialogues attributed to the man-god Hermes Trismegistus—the honorific title of "thrice-greatest Hermes," which the Greeks bestowed upon the Egyptian god of intellect Thoth, whom they venerated above their own Hermes.

These unsigned tracts became broadly known as the Hermetica. When rediscovered and translated by

Renaissance scholars, the Hermetic texts, covering philosophic, magical, alchemical, and occult ideas, formed an essential part of the Renaissance outlook, and shaped elements of scientific and rational thought associated with the Age of Enlightenment—an era that would soon relegate Hermeticism to the fringes of history, treating it as little more than a curio of late-Greek mystical thought.

But the Hermetica represents far more than that, a fact Atkinson understood and placed on display in *The Kybalion*. History, especially religious history, is an admixture of crosscurrents, frictions, and influences. The value of the Hermetica is that it preserves a sample of Egyptian thought, enfolded within Greek literary style and intermingled with Neo-Platonic and Hellenic philosophy. This is of immense importance, since our insight into Ancient Egyptian thought, which was often passed on through oral tradition or encoded in hieroglyphs and myths, is limited. Indeed, until very recently, we possessed few serviceable translations of the Hermetic literature, which was neglected after the Renaissance.

In *The Kybalion*, Atkinson expertly and artfully, using the few Victorian-era translations available to him, summarized the metaphysical psychology of the Hermetica, and combined it with his own insights into

New Thought, or what William James termed "the religion of healthy mindedness." The occult revival of the late-nineteenth century and the New Thought flowering of Atkinson's own era, provided the writer-publisher a perfect moment to reinterpret Hermetic ideas for a popular audience.

Hermeticism is not exactly the religious ancestor to New Thought. The paucity of translations and the rural surroundings of most of America's New Thought pioneers placed these ideas off their path. Early New Thoughters were largely independent investigators and reached their insights about the mind's causative abilities chiefly through self-experiment. But aspects of Hermeticism do represent a distant historical parallel to New Thought, especially Hermeticism's core idea that a Great Mind of Creation brought all things into being, and that this same creative mental faculty dwells in all men, beings the Higher Mind created not only in its own image but to function in its own likeness.

". . . your mind is god the father; they are not divided from one another for their union is life," says the Hermetica. This statement would be at home in any New Thought book.

Atkinson brilliantly surmises the possibilities—and limits—of the mind's power for earthbound men and women. If it were somehow possible for contemporary metaphysical seekers to reach back in time and have an exchange with the ancient Hermeticists, something like *The Kybalion* is probably as good an estimation as we can venture of what would appear.

I have reread *The Kybalion* many times, and encourage all who encounter these words to do so. But I have created this shortened version for several reasons: Brief as the original book is, its opening chapters present a detailed casebook in the nature of mental causation and the immaterial basis of reality—ideas that are perhaps more readily accepted today than in Atkinson's generation, and some readers may find his lawyerly style of argumentation a barrier to entry. That barrier has been somewhat eased in this abridgement, but without sacrificing any of his ideas. I have also shortened some of Atkinson's more speculative investigations—and I think he would have agreed that they were such—into the figurative nature of various corresponding planes of reality. I have also reduced the verbiage of certain arguments, in which he restated, as any good lawyer would, certain key premises.

The result, I hope, is an abridgement that retains the overall mission and, above all, the practicality of Atkinson's original. This digest-sized edition is not a substitute for the original, but it is an excellent entry point for the newcomer and, perhaps most importantly, a way for longtime readers and lovers of the book to re-experience or remind themselves of key points.

Most importantly, it falls to you, the reader and listener, to enact and experience these ideas in your life. "For otherwise," the book counsels, "the Hermetic Teachings will be as 'words, words, words' to you."

—Mitch Horowitz

We take great pleasure in presenting to the attention of students and investigators of the Secret Doctrines this little work based upon the world-old Hermetic Teachings.

The purpose of this work is not the enunciation of any special philosophy or doctrine, but rather is to give to the students a statement of the Truth that will serve to reconcile the many bits of occult knowledge that they may have acquired, but which are apparently opposed to each other and which often serve to discourage the beginner in the study. Our intent is not to erect a new Temple of Knowledge, but rather to place in the hands of the student a Master-Key with which he may open the many inner doors in the Temple of Mystery through the main portals he has already entered.

There is no portion of the occult teachings possessed by the world which have been so closely guarded as the fragments of the Hermetic Teachings, which have come down to us over the tens of centuries that have elapsed since the lifetime of its great founder, Hermes Trismegistus, the "scribe of the gods," who dwelt in old Egypt in the days when the present race of men was in its infancy. Contemporary with Abraham, and, if the legends be true, an instructor of that venerable sage, Hermes was, and is, the Great Central Sun of Occultism, whose rays have served to illumine the countless teachings which have been promulgated since his time. All the fundamental and basic teachings embedded in the esoteric teachings of every race may be traced back to Hermes.

The original truths taught by him have been kept intact in their original purity by a few men in each age who followed the Hermetic custom and reserved their truth for the few who were ready to comprehend and master it. From lip to ear, the truth has been handed down among the few. There have always been Initiates in each generation, in the various lands of the earth, who kept alive the sacred flame of the Hermetic Teachings. These men have never sought popular approval, nor numbers of followers. They are indifferent to these things, for they know how few there are in each generation who are ready for the truth, or who would recognize it if it were presented to them. They reserve the "strong meat for men," while others furnish the "milk for babes."

In this little work, we have endeavored to give you an idea of the fundamental teachings of *The Kybalion*, striving to give you the working Principles, leaving you to apply them yourselves, rather than attempting to work out the teaching in detail. If you are a true student, you will be able to work out and apply these Principles—if not, then you must develop yourself into one, for otherwise the Hermetic Teachings will be as "words, words, words" to you.

—Three Initiates

CHAPTER ONE

The Hermetic Philosophy

"The lips of wisdom are closed, except to the ears of Understanding." —THE KYBALION

From old Egypt have come the fundamental esoteric and occult teachings, which have so strongly influenced the philosophies of all races, nations, and peoples, for several thousand years. Egypt, the home of the Pyramids and the Sphinx, was the birthplace of the Hidden Wisdom and Mystic Teachings. From her Secret Doctrine all nations have borrowed. India, Persia, Chaldea, Medea, China, Japan, Assyria, ancient Greece and Rome, and other ancient countries partook liberally at the feast of knowledge which the Hierophants and Masters of the Land of Isis so freely provided for those who came prepared to partake of the great store of Mystic and Occult Lore which the masterminds of that ancient land had gathered together.

Among these great Masters of Ancient Egypt there once dwelt one whom Masters hailed as "The Master of Masters." This man, if "man" indeed he was, dwelt in Egypt in the earliest days. He was known as Hermes Trismegistus. He was the father of the Occult Wisdom; the founder of Astrology; the discoverer of Alchemy. The details of his life are lost to history, owing to the lapse of the years, though several of the ancient countries disputed with each other in their claims to the honor of having furnished his birthplace—and this thousands of years ago. The date of his sojourn in Egypt, in his last incarnation on this planet, is not now known, but it has been fixed at the early days of the oldest dynasties of Egypt—long before the days of Moses.

The Egyptians deified Hermes, and made him one of their gods, under the name of Thoth. Years after, the people of Ancient Greece also made him one of their many gods—calling him "Hermes, the god of Wisdom." The Egyptians revered his memory for many centuries, calling him "the Scribe of the Gods," and bestowing upon him, distinctively, his ancient title, "Trismegistus," which means "the thrice-great."

In the early days, there was a compilation of certain Basic Hermetic Doctrines, passed on from teacher to student, which was known as "THE KYBALION," the exact significance and meaning of the term having been lost for several centuries. This teaching, however, is known to many to whom it has descended, from mouth to ear, on and on throughout the centuries. Its precepts have never been written down, or printed, so far as we know. It was merely a collection of maxims, axioms, and precepts, which were non-understandable to outsiders, but which were readily understood by students, after the axioms, maxims, and precepts had been explained and exemplified by the Hermetic Initiates to their Neophytes. These teachings really constituted the basic principles of "The Art of Hermetic Alchemy," which, contrary to the general belief, dealt in the mastery of Mental Forces, rather than Material Elements—the Transmutation of one kind of Mental Vibrations into others, instead of the changing of one kind of metal into another. The legends of the "Philosopher's Stone," which would turn base metal into Gold, was an allegory relating to Hermetic Philosophy, readily understood by all students of true Hermeticism.

In this little book, of which this is the First Lesson, we invite our students to examine into the Hermetic Teachings, as set forth in THE KYBALION, and as explained by ourselves, humble students of the Teachings, who, while bearing the title of Initiates, are still students at the feet of HERMES, the Master.

The original maxims, axioms, and precepts of THE KYBALION are printed herein, in quotation marks. Our own work is printed in the regular way, in the body of the work. We trust that the many students to whom we now offer this little work will derive as much benefit from the study of its pages as have the many who have gone on before.

In the words of THE KYBALION:

> *"Where fall the footsteps of the Master, the ears of those ready for his Teaching open wide."*
> —THE KYBALION

> *"When the ears of the student are ready to hear, then cometh the lips to fill them with Wisdom."*
> —THE KYBALION

So that according to the Teachings, the passage of this book to those ready for the instruction will attract the attention of such as are prepared to receive the Teaching. And, likewise, when the pupil is ready to receive the truth, then will this little book come to him or her. Such is The Law. The Hermetic Principle of Cause and Effect, in its aspect of the Law of Attraction, will bring lips and ear together—pupil and book in company.

CHAPTER TWO

The Seven Hermetic Principles

"The Principles of Truth are Seven; he who knows these, understandingly, possesses the Magic Key before whose touch all the Doors of the Temple fly open." —THE KYBALION

The Seven Hermetic Principles, upon which the entire Hermetic Philosophy is based, are as follows:

I. THE PRINCIPLE OF MENTALISM
II. THE PRINCIPLE OF CORRESPONDENCE
III. THE PRINCIPLE OF VIBRATION
IV. THE PRINCIPLE OF POLARITY
V. THE PRINCIPLE OF RHYTHM
VI. THE PRINCIPLE OF CAUSE AND EFFECT
VII. THE PRINCIPLE OF GENDER

These Seven Principles will be discussed and explained as we proceed with these lessons. A short explanation of each, however, may be given at this point.

I. The Principle of Mentalism

"THE ALL IS MIND; The Universe is Mental."
—THE KYBALION

This Principle embodies the truth that "All is Mind." It explains that THE ALL (which is the Substantial Reality underlying all the outward manifestations and appearances which we know under the terms of "The Material Universe;" the "Phenomena of Life;" "Matter;" "Energy;" and, in short, all that is apparent to our material senses) is SPIRIT, which in itself is UNKNOWABLE and UNDEFINABLE, but which may be considered and thought of as A UNIVERSAL, INFINITE, LIVING MIND. It also explains that all the phenomenal world or universe is simply a Mental Creation of THE ALL, subject to the Laws of Created Things, and that the universe, as a whole, and in its parts or units, has its existence in the Mind of THE ALL, in which Mind we "live and move and have our being." This Principle explains the true nature of "Energy," "Power," and

"Matter," and why and how all these are subordinate to the Mastery of Mind. One of the old Hermetic Masters wrote, long ages ago: "He who grasps the truth of the Mental Nature of the Universe is well advanced on The Path to Mastery."

II. The Principle of Correspondence

"As above, so below; as below, so above."
—THE KYBALION

This Principle embodies the truth that there is always a Correspondence between the laws and phenomena of the various planes of Being and Life. The old Hermetic axiom ran in these words: "As above, so below; as below, so above." And the grasping of this Principle gives one the means of solving many a dark paradox and hidden secret of Nature. There are planes beyond our knowing, but when we apply the Principle of Correspondence to them we are able to understand much that would otherwise be unknowable to us. This Principle is of universal application and manifestation on the various planes of the material, mental, and spiritual universe—it is a Universal Law.

III. The Principle of Vibration

"Nothing rests; everything moves; everything vibrates."   —THE KYBALION

This Principle embodies the truth that "everything is in motion;" "everything vibrates;" "nothing is at rest;" facts which Modern Science endorses, and which each new scientific discovery tends to verify. From THE ALL, which is Pure Spirit, down to the grossest form of Matter, all is in vibration—the higher the vibration, the higher the position in the scale. The vibration of Spirit is at such an infinite rate of intensity and rapidity that it is practically at rest—just as a rapidly moving wheel seems to be motionless. At the other end of the scale, there are gross forms of matter whose vibrations are so low as to seem at rest. Between these poles are millions upon millions of varying degrees of vibration. From corpuscle and electron, atom and molecule, to worlds and universes, everything is in vibratory motion. An understanding of this Principle, with the appropriate formulas, enables Hermetic students to control their own mental vibrations as well as those of others. The Masters also apply this Principle to the conquering of Natural phenomena, in various ways. "He who understands the Principle of Vibration, has grasped the scepter of power," says one of the old writers.

IV. The Principle of Polarity

"Everything is Dual; everything has poles; every-thing has its pair of opposites; like and unlike are the same; opposites are identical in nature, but different in degree; extremes meet; all truths are but half-truths; all paradoxes may be reconciled."
—THE KYBALION

This Principle embodies the truth that "everything is dual;" "everything has two poles;" "everything has its pair of opposites," all of which were old Hermetic axi-oms. It explains the old paradoxes, that have perplexed so many, which have been stated as follows: "Thesis and antithesis are identical in nature, but different in degree;" "opposites are the same, differing only in degree;" "the pairs of opposites may be reconciled;" "extremes meet;" "everything is and isn't, at the same time;" "all truths are but half-truths;" etc. It explains that in everything there are two poles, or opposite aspects, and that "oppo-sites" are really only the two extremes of the same thing, with many varying degrees between them. To illustrate: Heat and Cold, although "opposites," are really the same thing, the differences consisting merely of degrees. Look at your thermometer and see if you can discover where "heat" terminates and "cold" begins! There is no such thing as "absolute heat" or "absolute cold"—the two terms simply indicate varying degrees of the same thing, and that "same thing" that manifests as "heat" and "cold" is merely a form, variety, and rate of Vibration. The same Principle manifests in the case of "Light and Darkness," which are the same thing, the difference consisting of varying degrees between the two poles of the phenomena. What is the difference between "Large and Small?" Between "Hard and Soft?" Between "Black and White?" Between "Sharp and Dull?" Between "Noise and Quiet?" Between "High and Low?" Between "Positive and Negative?" The Principle of Polarity explains these paradoxes, and no other Principle can supersede it. The same Principle operates on the Mental Plane. Let us take a radical and extreme example—that of "Love and Hate," two mental states apparently totally different. And yet there are degrees of Hate and degrees of Love, and a middle point in which we use the terms "Like or Dislike," which shade into each other so gradually that sometimes we are at a loss to know whether we "like" or "dislike" or "neither." All are simply degrees of the same thing, as you will see if you will but think a moment. And, more than this (and considered of more importance by the Hermetists), it is possible to change the vibrations of Hate to the vibrations of Love, in one's own mind, and in the minds of others. Many of you, who read these lines, have had personal experiences of the involuntary rapid transition from Love to Hate, and the reverse, in your own case and that of others. And you will therefore realize the possibility of this being accomplished by the use of the Will, by means of the Hermetic formulas. "Good and Evil" are but the poles of the same thing, and the Hermetist understands the art of transmuting Evil into Good, by means of an application of the Principle of Polarity. In short, the "Art of Polarization" becomes a phase of "Mental Alchemy" known and practiced by the ancient and modern Hermetic Masters. An understanding of the Principle will enable one to change his own Polarity, as well as that of others, if he will devote the time and study necessary to master the art.

V. The Principle of Rhythm

"Everything flows, out and in; everything has its tides; all things rise and fall; the pendulum-swing manifests in everything; the measure of the swing to the right is the measure of the swing to the left; rhythm compensates." —THE KYBALION

This Principle embodies the truth that in everything there is manifested a measured motion, to and fro; a

flow and inflow; a swing backward and forward; a pendulum-like movement; a tide-like ebb and flow; a high-
tide and low-tide; between the two poles which exist
in accordance with the Principle of Polarity described
a moment ago. There is always an action and a reaction; an advance and a retreat; a rising and a sinking.
The Hermetists have grasped this Principle, finding its
universal application, and have also discovered certain
means to overcome its effects in themselves by the use
of the appropriate formulas and methods. They apply
the Mental Law of Neutralization. They cannot annul
the Principle, or cause it to cease its operation, but they
have learned how to escape its effects upon themselves
to a certain degree depending upon the Mastery of the
Principle. They have learned how to USE it, instead of
being USED BY it. The Master of Hermetics polarizes
himself at the point at which he desires to rest, and then
neutralizes the Rhythmic swing of the pendulum which
would tend to carry him to the other pole. All individuals who have attained any degree of Self-Mastery do
this to a certain degree, more or less unconsciously, but
the Master does this consciously, and by the use of his
Will, and attains a degree of Poise and Mental Firmness
almost impossible of belief on the part of the masses
who are swung backward and forward like a pendulum.

VI. The Principle of Cause and Effect

"Every Cause has its Effect; every Effect has its Cause; everything happens according to Law; Chance is but a name for Law not recognized; there are many planes of causation, but nothing escapes the Law."   —THE KYBALION

This Principle embodies the fact that there is a Cause for every Effect; an Effect from every Cause. It explains that: "Everything Happens according to Law;" that nothing ever "merely happens;" that there is no such thing as Chance; that while there are various planes of Cause and Effect, the higher dominating the lower planes, still nothing ever entirely escapes the Law. The masses of people are carried along, obedient to environment; the wills and desires of others stronger than themselves; heredity; suggestion; and other outward causes moving them about like pawns on the Chessboard of Life. But the Masters, rising to the plane above, dominate their moods, characters, qualities, and powers, as well as the environment surrounding them, and become Movers instead of pawns. They help to PLAY THE GAME OF LIFE, instead of being played and moved about by other wills and environment. They

USE the Principle instead of being its tools. The Masters obey the Causation of the higher planes, but they help to RULE on their own plane. In this statement there is condensed a wealth of Hermetic knowledge—let him read who can.

VII. The Principle of Gender

"Gender is in everything; everything has its Masculine and Feminine Principles; Gender manifests on all planes." —THE KYBALION

This Principle embodies the truth that there is GENDER manifested in everything—the Masculine and Feminine Principles ever at work. This is true not only of the Physical Plane, but of the Mental and even the Spiritual Planes. On the Physical Plane, the Principle manifests as SEX, on the higher planes it takes higher forms, but the Principle is ever the same. No creation, physical, mental or spiritual, is possible without this Principle. An understanding of its laws will throw light on many a subject that has perplexed the minds of men. Everything, and every person, contains the two Elements or Principles, or this great Principle, within it, him or her. Every Male thing has the Female Element also; every Female contains also the Male Principle. If you would understand the philosophy of Mental and Spiritual Creation, Generation, and Re-generation, you must understand and study this Hermetic Principle. It contains the solution of many mysteries of Life.

CHAPTER THREE

Mental Transmutation

"Mind (as well as metals and elements) may be transmuted, from state to state; degree to degree; condition to condition; pole to pole; vibration to vibration. True Hermetic Transmutation is a Mental Art." —THE KYBALION

Mental Transmutation" means the art of changing and transforming mental states, forms, and conditions, into others. So you may see that Mental Transmutation is the "Art of Mental Chemistry," if you like the term—a form of practical Mystic Psychology.

But this means far more than appears on the surface. Transmutation, Alchemy, or Chemistry, on the Mental Plane is important enough in its effects, to be sure, and if the art stopped there it would still be one of the most important branches of study known to man. But this is only the beginning. Let us see why!

The first of the Seven Hermetic Principles is the Principle of Mentalism, the axiom of which is "THE ALL is Mind; the Universe is Mental," which means that the Underlying Reality of the Universe is Mind; and the Universe itself is Mental— that is, "existing in the Mind of THE ALL." We shall consider this Principle in succeeding lessons, but let us see the effect of the principle if it be assumed to be true.

If the Universal is Mental in its nature, then Mental Transmutation must be the art of CHANGING THE CONDITIONS OF THE UNIVERSE, along the lines of Matter, Force, and Mind. So you see, therefore, that Mental Transmutation is really the "Magic" of which the ancient writers had so much to say in their mystical works, and about which they gave so few practical instructions. If All be Mental, then the art which enables one to transmute mental conditions must render the Master the controller of material conditions as well as those ordinarily called "mental."

None but advanced Mental Alchemists have been able to attain the degree of power necessary to control the grosser physical conditions, such as the control of the elements of Nature.

But students and Hermetists of lesser degree than Masters—the Initiates and Teachers—are able to freely work along the Mental Plane, in Mental Transmutation. In fact all that we call "psychic phenomena;" "mental influence;" "mental science;" "new-thought phenomena;" etc., operates along the same general lines, for there is but one principle involved, no matter by what name the phenomena be called.

The student and practitioner of Mental Transmutation works among the Mental Plane, transmuting mental conditions, states, etc., into others. Not only may the mental states, etc., of one's self be changed or transmuted by Hermetic Methods; but also the states of others may be, and are, constantly transmuted in the same way, usually unconsciously.

We shall now proceed to a consideration of the first of the Hermetic Seven Principles—the Principle of Mentalism, in which is explained the truth that "THE ALL is Mind; the Universe is Mental," in the words of The Kybalion. We ask the close attention, and careful study of this great Principle, on the part of our students, for it is really the Basic Principle of the whole Hermetic Philosophy.

CHAPTER FOUR

The Mental Universe

"The Universe is Mental—held in the Mind of THE ALL." —THE KYBALION

THE ALL is SPIRIT! But what is Spirit? This question cannot be answered, for the reason that its definition is practically that of THE ALL, which cannot be explained or defined. Spirit is simply a name that men give to the highest conception of Infinite Living Mind—it means "the Real Essence"—it means Living Mind, as much superior to Life and Mind as we know them, as the latter are superior to mechanical Energy and Matter. Spirit transcends our understanding, and we use the term merely that we may think or speak of THE ALL. For the purposes of thought and understanding, we are justified in thinking of Spirit as Infinite Living Mind, at the same time acknowledging that we cannot fully understand it.

Let us now proceed to a consideration of the nature of the Universe, as a whole and in its parts. What is the Universe? We have seen that there can be nothing outside of THE ALL. Then is the Universe THE ALL? No, this cannot be, because the Universe seems to be made up of MANY, and is constantly changing, and in other ways it does not measure up to the ideas that we are compelled to accept regarding THE ALL, as stated in our last lesson. Then if the Universe be not THE ALL, then it must be Nothing—such is the inevitable conclusion of the mind at first thought. But this will not satisfy the question, for we are sensible of the existence of the Universe. Then if the Universe is neither THE ALL, nor Nothing, what can it be? Let us examine this question.

If the Universe exists at all, or seems to exist, it must proceed in some way from THE ALL—it must be a creation of THE ALL. But as something can never come from nothing, from what could THE ALL have created it? Some philosophers have answered this question by saying that THE ALL created the Universe from ITSELF—that is, from the being and substance of THE ALL. But this will not do, for THE ALL cannot be subtracted from, nor divided, as we have seen, and then again if this be so, would not each particle in the Universe be aware of its being THE ALL—THE ALL could not lose its knowledge of itself, nor actually BECOME an atom, or blind force, or lowly living thing.

But, what indeed is the Universe, if it be not THE ALL, yet not created by THE ALL having separated itself into fragments? What else can it be—of what else can it be made? This is the great question. Let us examine it carefully. We find that the "Principle of Correspondence" comes to our aid here. The old Hermetic axiom, "As above so below," may be pressed into service at this point. Let us endeavor to get a glimpse of the workings on higher planes by examining those on our own. The Principle of Correspondence must apply to this as well as to other problems.

On his own plane of being, how does Man create? He CREATES MENTALLY! And in so doing he uses no outside materials, nor does he reproduce himself, and yet his Spirit pervades the Mental Creation.

Following the Principle of Correspondence, we are justified in considering that THE ALL creates the Universe MENTALLY, in a manner akin to the process whereby Man creates Mental Images. THE ALL can create in no other way except mentally, without either using material (and there is none to use), or else reproducing itself (which is also impossible). There is no escape from this conclusion of the Reason, which agrees with the highest teachings of the Illumined. Just as you, student, may create a Universe of your own in your mentality, so does THE ALL create Universes in its own Mentality. But your Universe is the mental creation of a Finite Mind, whereas that of THE ALL is the creation of an Infinite. The two are similar in kind, but infinitely different in degree. We shall examine more closely into the process of creation and manifestation, as we proceed. But this is the point to fix in your minds at this stage: THE UNIVERSE, AND ALL IT CONTAINS, IS A MENTAL CREATION OF THE ALL. Verily, indeed, ALL IS MIND!

CHAPTER FIVE

The Divine Paradox

"The half-wise, recognizing the comparative unreality of the Universe, imagine that they may defy its Laws—such are vain and presumptuous fools, and they are broken against the rocks and torn asunder by the elements by reason of their folly. The truly wise, knowing the nature of the Universe, use Law against laws; the higher against the lower; and by the Art of Alchemy transmute that which is undesirable into that which is worthy, and thus triumph. Mastery consists not in abnormal dreams, visions, and fantastic imaginings or living, but in using the higher forces against the lower—escaping the pains of the lower planes by vibrating on the higher. Transmutation, not presumptuous denial, is the weapon of the Master."
—THE KYBALION

This is the Paradox of the Universe, resulting from the Principle of Polarity which manifests when THE ALL begins to Create—hearken to it for it points the difference between half-wisdom and wisdom. While to THE INFINITE ALL, the Universe, its Laws, its Powers, its Life, its Phenomena, are as things witnessed in the state of Meditation or Dream; yet to all that is Finite, the Universe must be treated as Real, and life and action and thought, must be based thereupon, accordingly, although with an ever understanding of the Higher Truth. Each according to its own Plane and Laws. If Man, owing to half-wisdom, acts and lives and thinks of the Universe as merely a dream (akin to his own finite dreams) then indeed does it so become for him, and like a sleep-walker he stumbles ever around and around in a circle, making no progress, and being forced into an awakening at last by his falling bruised and bleeding over the Natural Laws which he ignored. Keep your mind ever on the Star, but let your eyes watch over your footsteps, lest you fall into the mire by reason of your upward gaze. Remember the Divine Paradox that while the Universe IS NOT, still IT IS. Remember ever the Two Poles of Truth—the Absolute and the Relative. Beware of Half-Truths.

What Hermetists know as "the Law of Paradox" is an aspect of the Principle of Polarity. The Hermetic writings are filled with references to the appearance of the Paradox in the consideration of the problems of Life and Being. The Teachers are constantly warning their students against the error of omitting the "other side" of any question. And their warnings are particularly directed to the problems of the Absolute and the Relative, which perplex all students of philosophy, and which cause so many to think and act contrary to what is generally known as "common sense." And we caution all students to be sure to grasp the Divine Paradox of the Absolute and Relative, lest they become entangled in the mire of the Half-Truth. With this in view this particular lesson has been written. Read it carefully!

The first thought that comes to the thinking man after he realizes the truth that the Universe is a Mental Creation of THE ALL, is that the Universe and all that it contains is a mere illusion; an unreality; against which idea his instincts revolt. But this, like all other great truths, must be considered both from the Absolute and the Relative points of view. From the Absolute viewpoint, of course, the Universe is in the nature of an illusion, a dream, a phantasmagoria, as compared to THE ALL in itself. We recognize this even in our ordinary view, for we speak of the world as "a fleeting show" that comes and goes, is born and dies—for the element of impermanence and change, finiteness and unsubstantiality, must ever be connected with the idea of a created Universe when it is contrasted with the idea of THE ALL.

Anything that has a beginning and an ending must be, in a sense, unreal and untrue, and the Universe comes under that rule, in all schools of thought. From the Absolute point of view, there is nothing Real except THE ALL.

But the Absolute point of view shows merely one side of the picture—the other side is the Relative one. Absolute Truth has been defined as, "Things as the mind of God knows them," while Relative Truth is, "Things as the highest reason of Man understands them." And so while to THE ALL the Universe must be unreal and illusionary, a mere dream or result of meditation—nevertheless, to the finite minds forming a part of that Universe, and viewing it through mortal faculties, the Universe is very real indeed, and must be so considered. In recognizing the Absolute view, we must not make the mistake of ignoring or denying the facts and phenomena of the Universe as they present themselves to our mortal faculties—we are not THE ALL, remember.

To take familiar illustrations, we all recognize that Matter "exists" to our senses—we will fare badly if we do not. And yet, even our finite minds understand the scientific dictum that there is no such thing as Matter from a scientific point of view—that which we call Matter is held to be merely an aggregation of atoms, which atoms themselves are merely a grouping of units of force, vibrating and in constant circular motion. We kick a stone and we feel the impact—it seems to be real, notwithstanding that we know it to be merely what we have stated above. But remember that our foot, which feels the impact by means of our brains, is likewise Matter, so constituted of electrons, and for that matter so are our brains. And, at the best, if it were not by reason of our Mind, we would not know the foot or stone at all.

Oh, friends, to mortals this Universe of Mentality is very real indeed—it is the only one we can ever know, though we rise from plane to plane, higher and higher in it. To know it otherwise, by actual experience, we must be THE ALL itself. It is true that the higher we rise in the scale—the nearer to "the mind of the Father" we reach—the more apparent becomes the illusory nature of finite things, but not until THE ALL finally withdraws us into itself does the vision actually vanish.

So, we need not dwell upon the feature of illusion. Rather let us, recognizing the real nature of the Universe, seek to understand its mental laws, and endeavor to use them to the best effect in our upward progress through life, as we travel from plane to plane of being. The Laws of the Universe are nonetheless "Iron Laws" because of the mental nature. All, except THE ALL, are bound by them. What is IN THE INFINITE

MIND OF THE ALL is REAL in a degree second only to that Reality itself which is vested in the nature of THE ALL.

The Hermetic Principle of Mentalism, while explaining the true nature of the Universe upon the principle that all is Mental, does not change the scientific conceptions of the Universe, Life, or Evolution. So, the student of Hermetics need not lay aside any of his cherished scientific views regarding the Universe. All he is asked to do is to grasp the underlying principle of, "THE ALL is Mind; the Universe is Mental—held in the Mind of THE ALL." He will find that the other six of the Seven Principles will "fit into" his scientific knowledge, and will serve to bring out obscure points and to throw light in dark corners.

The purpose of this lesson is to impress upon the minds of our students the fact that, to all intents and purposes, the Universe and its laws, and its phenomena, are just as REAL, so far as Man is concerned, as they would be under the hypotheses of Materialism or Energism. Under any hypothesis the Universe in its outer aspect is changing, everflowing, and transitory— and therefore devoid of substantiality and reality. But (note the other pole of the truth) under any of the same hypotheses, we are compelled to ACT AND LIVE as if the fleeting things were real and substantial. With this difference, always, between the various hypotheses—that under the old views Mental Power was ignored as a Natural Force, while under Mentalism it becomes the Greatest Natural Force. And this one difference revolutionizes Life, to those who understand the Principle and its resulting laws and practice.

Chapter Six

The Planes of Correspondence

"As above, so below; as below, so above."
—The Kybalion

The great Second Hermetic Principle embodies the truth that there is a harmony, agreement, and correspondence between the several planes of Manifestation, Life, and Being. This truth is a truth because all that is included in the Universe emanates from the same source, and the same laws, principles, and characteristics apply to each unit, or combination of units of activity, as each manifests its own phenomena upon its own plane.

For the purpose of convenience of thought and study, the Hermetic Philosophy considers that the Universe may be divided into three great classes of phenomena, known as the Three Great Planes, namely:

I. The Great Physical Plane
II. The Great Mental Plane
III. The Great Spiritual Plane

These divisions are more or less artificial and arbitrary, for the truth is that all of the three divisions are but ascending degrees of the great scale of Life, the lowest point of which is undifferentiated Matter, and the highest point that of Spirit. And, moreover, the different Planes shade into each other, so that no hard and fast division may be made between the higher phenomena of the Physical and the lower of the Mental.

You will kindly remember, however, that the Three Great Planes are not actual divisions of the phenomena of the Universe, but merely arbitrary terms used by the Hermetists in order to aid in the thought and study of the various degrees and forms of universal activity and life. The atom of matter, the unit of force, the mind of man, and the being of the archangel are all but degrees in one scale, and all fundamentally the same, the difference between solely a matter of degree, and rate of vibration—all are creations of THE ALL, and have their existence solely within the Infinite Mind of THE ALL.

We would again remind you that according to the Principle of Correspondence, which embodies the truth, "As Above so Below; as Below, so Above," all of the Seven Hermetic Principles are in full operation on all of the many planes, Physical, Mental and Spiritual. The Principle of Mental Substance, of course, applies to all the planes, for all are held in the Mind of THE ALL. The Principle of Correspondence manifests in all, for there is a correspondence, harmony, and agreement between the several planes. The Principle of Vibration manifests on all planes, in fact the very differences that go to make the "planes" arise from Vibration, as we have explained. The Principle of Polarity manifests on each plane, the extremes of the Poles being apparently opposite and contradictory. The Principle of Rhythm manifests on each Plane, the movement of the phenomena having its ebb and flow, rise and flow, incoming and outgoing. The Principle of Cause and Effect manifests on each Plane, every Effect having its Cause and every Cause having its effect. The Principle of Gender manifests on each Plane, the Creative Energy being always manifest, and operating along the lines of its Masculine and Feminine Aspects.

"As Above so Below; as Below, so Above." This centuries old Hermetic axiom embodies one of the great Principles of Universal Phenomena. As we proceed with our consideration of the remaining Principles, we will see even more clearly the truth of the universal nature of this great Principle of Correspondence.

CHAPTER SEVEN

Vibration

"Nothing rests; everything moves; everything vibrates."
— THE KYBALION

The great Third Hermetic Principle—the Principle of Vibration—embodies the truth that Motion is manifest in everything in the Universe—that nothing is at rest—that everything moves, vibrates, and circles.

The Hermetic Teachings are that not only is everything in constant movement and vibration, but that the "differences" between the various manifestations of the universal power are due entirely to the varying rate and mode of vibrations. Not only this, but that even THE ALL, in itself, manifests a constant vibration of such an infinite degree of intensity and rapid motion that it may be practically considered as at rest, the teachers directing the attention of the students to the fact that even on the physical plane a rapidly moving object (such as a revolving wheel) seems to be at rest. The Teachings are to the effect that Spirit is at one end of the Pole of Vibration, the other Pole being certain extremely gross forms of Matter. Between these two poles are millions upon millions of different rates and modes of vibration.

Scientists have offered the illustration of a rapidly moving wheel, top, or cylinder, to show the effects of increasing rates of vibration. The illustration supposes a wheel, top, or revolving cylinder, running at a low rate of speed—we will call this revolving thing "the object" in following out the illustration. Let us suppose the object moving slowly. It may be seen readily, but no sound of its movement reaches the ear. The speed is gradually increased. In a few moments its movement becomes so rapid that a deep growl or low note may be heard. Then as the rate is increased the note rises one in the musical scale. Then, the motion being still further increased, the next highest note is distinguished. Then, one after another, all the notes of the musical scale appear, rising higher and higher as the motion is increased. Finally, when the motions have reached a certain rate the final note perceptible to human ears is reached and the shrill, piercing shriek dies away, and silence follows. No sound is heard from the revolving object, the rate of motion being so high that the human ear cannot register the vibrations. Then comes the perception of rising degrees of Heat.

When the object reaches a certain rate of vibration its molecules disintegrate, and resolve themselves into the original elements or atoms. Then the atoms, following the Principle of Vibration, are separated into the countless corpuscles of which they are composed. And, finally, even the corpuscles disappear and the object may be said to be composed of The Ethereal Substance. Science does not dare to follow the illustration further, but the Hermetists teach that if the vibrations be continually increased the object would mount up the successive states of manifestation and would in turn manifest the various mental stages, and then on Spiritward, until it would finally reenter THE ALL, which is Absolute Spirit.

The Hermetic Teachings go much further than do those of modern science. They teach that all manifestation of thought, emotion, reason, will or desire, or any mental state or condition, are accompanied by vibrations, a portion of which are thrown off, and which tend to affect the minds of other persons by "induction." This is the principle which produces the phenomena of "telepathy;" mental influence, and other forms of the action and power of mind over mind. Every thought, emotion or mental state has its corresponding rate and mode of vibration. And by an effort of the will of the person, or of other persons, these mental states may be reproduced, just as a musical tone may be reproduced by causing an instrument to vibrate at a certain rate—just as color may be reproduced in the same way. By a knowledge of the Principle of Vibration, as applied to Mental Phenomena, one may polarize his mind at any degree he wishes, thus gaining a perfect control over his mental states, moods, etc. In the same way he may affect the minds of others, producing the desired mental states in them. In short, he may be able to produce on the Mental Plane that which science produces on the Physical Plane—namely, "Vibrations at Will."

A little reflection on what we have said will show the student that the Principle of Vibration underlies the wonderful phenomena of the power manifested by the Masters and Adepts, who are able to apparently set aside the Laws of Nature, but who, in reality, are simply using one law against another; one principle against others; and who accomplish their results by changing the vibrations of material objects, or forms of energy, and thus perform what are commonly called "miracles."

As one of the old Hermetic writers has truly said: "He who understands the Principle of Vibration, has grasped the scepter of Power."

CHAPTER EIGHT

Polarity

"Everything is dual; everything has poles; everything has its pair of opposites; like and unlike are the same; opposites are identical in nature, but different in degree; extremes meet; all truths are but half-truths; all paradoxes may be reconciled."
—THE KYBALION

The great Fourth Hermetic Principle—the Principle of Polarity—embodies the truth that all manifested things have "two sides;" "two aspects;" "two poles;" a "pair of opposites," with manifold degrees between the two extremes. The old paradoxes, which have ever perplexed the mind of men, are explained by an understanding of this Principle. Man has always recognized something akin to this Principle.

The Hermetic Teachings are to the effect that the difference between things seemingly diametrically opposed to each other is merely a matter of degree. It teaches that "the pairs of opposites may be reconciled," and that "thesis and anti-thesis are identical in nature, but different in degree," and that the "universal reconciliation of opposites" is affected by a recognition of this Principle of Polarity. The teachers claim that illustrations of this Principle may be had on every hand, and from an examination into the real nature of anything. They begin by showing that Spirit and Matter are but the two poles of the same thing, the intermediate planes being merely degrees of vibration. They show that THE ALL and The Many are the same, the difference being merely a matter of degree of Mental Manifestation.

Light and Darkness are poles of the same thing, with many degrees between them. The musical scale is the same—starting with "C" you move upward until you reach another "C," and so on, the differences between the two ends of the board being the same, with many degrees between the two extremes.

Good and Bad are not absolute—we call one end of the scale Good and the other Bad, or one end Good and the other Evil, according to the use of the terms. A thing is "less good" than the thing higher in the scale; but that "less good" thing, in turn, is "more good" than the thing next below it—and so on, the "more or less" being regulated by the position on the scale.

And so it is on the Mental Plane. "Love and Hate" are generally regarded as being things diametrically opposed to each other; entirely different; unreconcilable. But we apply the Principle of Polarity; we find that there is no such thing as Absolute Love or Absolute Hate, as distinguished from each other. The two are merely terms applied to the two poles of the same thing. The Pairs of Opposites exist everywhere. Where you find one thing you find its opposite—the two poles.

And it is this fact that enables the Hermetist to transmute one mental state into another, along the lines of Polarization. Things belonging to different classes cannot be transmuted into each other, but things of the same class may be changed, that is, may have their polarity changed. Thus Love never becomes East or West, or Red or Violet—but it may and often does turn into Hate—and likewise Hate may be transformed into Love, by changing its polarity. Courage may be transmuted into Fear, and the reverse. Hard things may be rendered Soft. Dull things become Sharp. Hot things become Cold. And so on, the transmutation always being between things of the same kind of different degrees. Take the case of a Fearful man. By raising his mental vibrations along the line of Fear-Courage, he can be filled with the highest degree of Courage and Fear-lessness. And, likewise, the Slothful man may change himself into an Active, Energetic individual, simply by polarizing along the lines of the desired quality.

The student who is familiar with the processes by which the various schools of Mental Science, etc., produce changes in the mental states of those following their teachings, may not readily understand the principle underlying many of these changes. When, however, the Principle of Polarity is once grasped, and it is seen that the mental changes are occasioned by a change of polarity—a sliding along the same scale—the matter is more readily understood. The change is not in the nature of a transmutation of one thing into another thing entirely different—but is merely a change of degree in the same things, a vastly important difference.

The student will readily recognize that in the mental states, as well as in the phenomena of the Physical Plane, the two poles may be classified as Positive and Negative, respectively. Thus Love is Positive to Hate; Courage to Fear; Activity to Non-Activity, etc. And it will also be noticed that even to those unfamiliar with the Principle of Vibration, the Positive pole seems to be of a higher degree than the Negative, and readily dominates it. The tendency of Nature is in the direction of the dominant activity of the Positive pole.

In addition to the changing of the poles of one's own mental states by the operation of the art of Polarization, the phenomena of Mental Influence, in its manifold phases, shows us that the principle may be extended so as to embrace the phenomena of the influence of one mind over that of another. When it is understood that Mental Induction is possible, that is that mental states may be produced by "induction" from others, then we can readily see how a certain rate of vibration, or polarization of a certain mental state, may be communicated to another person, and his polarity in that class of mental states thus changed. It is along this principle that the results of many of the "mental treatments" are obtained. For instance, a person is "blue," melancholy and full of fear. A mental scientist bringing his own mind up to the desired vibration by his trained will, and thus obtaining the desired polarization in his own case, then produces a similar mental state in the other by induction, the result being that the vibrations are raised and the person polarizes toward the Positive end of the scale instead toward the Negative, and his Fear and other negative emotions are transmuted to Courage and similar positive mental states. A little study will show you that these mental changes are nearly all along the line of Polarization, the change being one of degree rather than of kind.

A knowledge of the existence of this great Hermetic Principle will enable the student to better understand his own mental states, and those of other people. He will see that these states are all matters of degree, and seeing thus, he will be able to raise or lower the vibration at will—to change his mental poles, and thus be Master of his mental states, instead of being their servant and slave. And by his knowledge he will be able to aid his fellows intelligently, and by the appropriate methods change the polarity when the same is desirable. We advise all students to familiarize themselves with this Principle of Polarity, for a correct understanding of the same will throw light on many difficult subjects.

CHAPTER NINE

Rhythm

"Everything flows out and in; everything has its tides; all things rise and fall; the pendulum-swing manifests in everything; the measure of the swing to the right, is the measure of the swing to the left; rhythm compensates." —THE KYBALION

The great Fifth Hermetic Principle—the Principle of Rhythm—embodies the truth that in everything there is manifested a measured motion; a to-and-from movement; a flow and inflow; a swing forward and backward; a pendulum-like movement; a tide-like ebb and flow; a high-tide and a low-tide; between the two-poles manifest on the physical, mental or spiritual planes. The Principle of Rhythm is closely connected with the Principle of Polarity described in the preceding chapter. Rhythm manifests between the two poles established by the Principle of Polarity. This does not mean, however, that the pendulum of Rhythm swings to the extreme poles, for this rarely happens; in fact, it is difficult to establish the extreme polar opposites in the majority of cases. But the swing is ever "toward" first one pole and then the other.

There is always an action and reaction; an advance and a retreat; a rising and a sinking; manifested in all of the airs and phenomena of the Universe. Suns, worlds, men, animals, plants, minerals, forces, energy, mind and matter, yes, even Spirit, manifests this Principle. The Principle manifests in the creation and destruction of worlds; in the rise and fall of nations; in the life history of all things; and, finally, in the mental states of Man.

The Principle of Rhythm is well understood by modern science, and is considered a universal law as applied to material things. But the Hermetists carry the principle much further, and know that its manifestations and influence extend to the mental activities of Man, and that it accounts for the bewildering succession of moods, feelings, and other annoying and perplexing changes that we notice in ourselves. But the Hermetists by studying the operations of this Principle have learned to escape some of its activities by Transmutation.

The Hermetic Masters long since discovered that while the Principle of Rhythm was invariable, and ever in evidence in mental phenomena, still there were two planes of its manifestation so far as mental phenomena are concerned. They discovered that there were two general planes of Consciousness, the Lower and the Higher, the understanding of which enabled them to rise to the higher plane and thus escape the swing of the Rhythmic pendulum which manifested on the lower plane. In other words, the swing of the pendulum occurred on the Unconscious Plane, and the Consciousness was not affected. This they call the Law of Neutralization. Its operations consist in the raising of the Ego above the vibrations of the Unconscious Plane of mental activity, so that the negative-swing of the pendulum is not manifested in consciousness, and therefore they are not affected. It is akin to rising above a thing and letting it pass beneath you. The Hermetic Master, or advanced student, polarizes himself at the desired pole, and by a process akin to "refusing" to participate in the backward swing, or, if you prefer, a "denial" of its influence over him, he stands firm in his polarized position, and allows the mental pendulum to swing back along the unconscious plane. All individuals who have attained any degree of self-mastery, accomplish this, more or less unknowingly, and by refusing to allow their moods and

negative mental states to affect them, they apply the Law
of Neutralization. The Master, however, carries this to a
much higher degree of proficiency, and by the use of his
Will he attains a degree of Poise and Mental Firmness
almost impossible of belief on the part of those who
allow themselves to be swung backward and forward by
the mental pendulum of moods and feelings.

The importance of this will be appreciated by any
thinking person who realizes what creatures of moods,
feelings, and emotion the majority of people are, and
how little mastery of themselves they manifest. If you
will stop and consider a moment, you will realize how
much these swings of Rhythm have affected you in
your life—how a period of Enthusiasm has been invariably followed by an opposite feeling and mood of De-
pression. Likewise, your moods and periods of Courage
have been succeeded by equal moods of Fear. And so
it has ever been with the majority of persons—tides of
feeling have ever risen and fallen with them, but they
have never suspected the cause or reason of the mental phenomena. An understanding of the workings of
this Principle will give one the key to the Mastery of
these rhythmic swings of feeling, and will enable him to
know himself better, and to avoid being carried away by
these in flows and out flows. The Will is superior to the
conscious manifestation of this Principle, although the

Principle itself can never be destroyed. We may escape its effects, but the Principle operates, nevertheless. The pendulum ever swings, although we may escape being carried along with it.

There are other features of the operation of this Principle of Rhythm of which we wish to speak at this point. There comes into its operations that which is known as the Law of Compensation. One of the definitions or meanings of the word "Compensate" is "to counterbalance," which is the sense in which the Hermetists use the term. It is this Law of Compensation to which The Kybalion refers when it says: "The measure of the swing to the right is the measure of the swing to the left; rhythm compensates."

The Law of Compensation is that the swing in one direction determines the swing in the opposite direction, or to the opposite pole—the one balances, or counterbalances, the other. The pendulum, with a short swing in one direction, has but a short swing in the other; while the long swing to the right invariably means the long swing to the left. An object hurled upward to a certain height has an equal distance to traverse on its return. The force with which a projectile is sent upward a mile is reproduced when the projectile returns to the earth on its return journey. This Law is constant on the Physical Plane.

But the Hermetists carry it still further. They teach that a man's mental states are subject to the same Law. The man who enjoys keenly, is subject to keen suffering; while he who feels but little pain is capable of feeling but little joy.

There are temperaments which permit of but low degrees of enjoyment, and equally low degrees of suffering; while there are others which permit the most intense enjoyment, but also the most intense suffering. The rule is that the capacity for pain and pleasure, in each individual, are balanced. The Law of Compensation is in full operation here.

But the Hermetists go still further in this matter. They teach that before one is able to enjoy a certain degree of pleasure, he must have swung as far, proportionately, toward the other pole of feeling. They hold, however, that the Negative is precedent to the Positive in this matter, that is to say that in experiencing a certain degree of pleasure it does not follow that he will have to "pay up for it" with a corresponding degree of pain; on the contrary, the pleasure is the Rhythmic swing, according to the Law of Compensation, for a degree of pain previously experienced either in the present life, or in a previous incarnation. This throws a new light on the Problem of Pain.

The Hermetists claim that the Master or advanced student is able, to a great degree, to escape the swing toward Pain, by the process of Neutralization before mentioned. By rising on to the higher plane of the Ego, much of the experience that comes to those dwelling on the lower plane is avoided and escaped.

The Law of Compensation plays an important part in the lives of men and women. It will be noticed that one generally "pays the price" of anything he possesses or lacks. If he has one thing, he lacks another—the balance is struck. The things that one gains are always paid for by the things that one loses. And so it is through life. The Law of Compensation is ever in operation, striving to balance and counter-balance, and always succeeding in time, even though several lives may be required for the return swing of the Pendulum of Rhythm.

CHAPTER TEN

Causation

> *"Every Cause has its Effect; every Effect has its Cause; everything happens according to Law; Chance is but a name for Law not recognized; there are many planes of causation, but nothing escapes the Law."* —THE KYBALION

The great Sixth Hermetic Principle—the Principle of Cause and Effect—embodies the truth that Law pervades the Universe; that nothing happens by Chance; that Chance is merely a term indicating cause existing but not recognized or perceived; that phenomena is continuous, without break or exception.

A little consideration will show you that there can be no such agent as "Chance," in the sense of something outside of Law—something outside of Cause and

Effect. How could there be a something acting in the phenomenal universe, independent of the laws, order, and continuity of the latter? Such a something would be entirely independent of the orderly trend of the universe, and therefore superior to it. We can imagine nothing outside of THE ALL being outside of the Law, and that only because THE ALL is the LAW in itself. There is no room in the universe for a something outside of and independent of Law. The existence of such a Something would render all Natural Laws ineffective, and would plunge the universe into chaotic disorder and lawlessness.

What we call "Chance" is merely an expression relating to obscure causes; causes that we cannot perceive; causes that we cannot understand. The word Chance is derived from a word meaning "to fall" (as the falling of dice), the idea being that the fall of the dice (and many other happenings) are merely a "happening" unrelated to any cause. And this is the sense in which the term is generally employed. But when the matter is closely examined, it is seen that there is no chance whatsoever about the fall of the dice. Each time a die falls, and displays a certain number, it obeys a law as infallible as that which governs the revolution of the planets around the sun. Back of the fall of the die are causes, or chains of causes, running back further than the mind can follow. The position of the die in the box; the amount of muscular energy expended in the throw; the condition of the table, etc., all are causes, the effect of which may be seen. But back of these seen causes are chains of unseen preceding causes, all of which had a bearing upon the number of the die which fell uppermost.

If a die be cast a great number of times, it will be found that the numbers shown will be about equal, that is, there will be an equal number of one-spot, two-spot, etc., coming upper-most. Toss a penny in the air, and it may come down either "heads" or "tails;" but make a sufficient number of tosses, and the heads and tails will about even up. This is the operation of the law of average. But both the average and the single toss come under the Law of Cause and Effect, and if we were able to examine into the preceding causes, it would be clearly seen that it was simply impossible for the die to fall other than it did, under the same circumstances and at the same time. Given the same causes, the same results will follow. There is always a "cause" and a "because" to every event. Nothing ever "happens" without a cause, or rather a chain of causes.

There is a continuity between all events precedent, consequent, and subsequent. There is a relation existing between everything that has gone before, and everything that follows. Stop to think a moment. If a certain man had not met a certain maid, away back in the dim period of the Stone Age—you who are now reading these lines would not now be here. And if, perhaps, the same couple had failed to meet, we who now write these lines would not now be here. And the very act of writing, on our part, and the act of reading, on yours, will affect not only the respective lives of yourself and ourselves, but will also have a direct, or indirect, affect upon many other people now living and who will live in the ages to come. Every thought we think, every act we perform, has its direct and indirect results, which fit into the great chain of Cause and Effect.

We do not wish to enter into a consideration of Free-Will, or Determinism, in this work, for various reasons. Among the many reasons, is the principal one that neither side of the controversy is entirely right—in fact, both sides are partially right, according to the Hermetic Teachings. The Principle of Polarity shows that both are but Half-Truths—the opposing poles of Truth. The Teachings are that a man may be both Free and yet bound by Necessity, depending upon the meaning of the terms, and the height of Truth from which the matter is examined. The ancient writers express the matter thus: "The further the creation is from the Centre, the more it is bound; the nearer the Centre it reaches, the nearer Free is it."

The majority of people are more or less the slaves of heredity, environment, etc., and manifest very little Freedom. They are swayed by the opinions, customs and thoughts of the outside world, and also by their emotions, feelings, moods, etc. The majority of people are carried along like a falling stone, obedient to environment, outside influences and internal moods, desires, etc., not to speak of the desires and wills of others stronger than themselves, carrying them along without resistance on their part, or the exercise of the Will. Moved like the pawns on the checkerboard of life, they play their parts and are laid aside after the game is over. But the Masters, knowing the rules of the game, rise above the plane of material life, and placing themselves in touch with the higher powers of their nature, dominate their own moods, characters, qualities, and polarity, as well as the environment surrounding them, and thus become Movers in the game, instead of Pawns—Causes instead of Effects. The Masters do not escape the Causation of the higher planes, but fall in with the higher laws, and thus master circumstances on the lower plane. They thus form a conscious part of the Law, instead of being mere blind instruments.

While they Serve on the Higher Planes, they Rule on the Material Plane.

The Hermetic Teachings are that Man may use Law to overcome laws, and that the higher will always prevail against the lower, until at last he has reached the stage in which he seeks refuge in the LAW itself. Are you able to grasp the inner meaning of this?

CHAPTER ELEVEN

Gender

"Gender is in everything; everything has its Masculine and Feminine Principles; Gender manifests on all planes." —THE KYBALION

The great Seventh Hermetic Principle—the Principle of Gender—embodies the truth that there is Gender manifested in everything—that the Masculine and Feminine principles are ever present and active in all phases of phenomena, on each and every plane of life. At this point we think it well to call your attention to the fact that Gender, in its Hermetic sense, and Sex in the ordinarily accepted use of the term, are not the same.

The word "Gender" is derived from the Latin root meaning "to beget; to procreate; to generate; to create; to produce." A moment's consideration will show you that the word has a much broader and more general meaning than the term "Sex," the latter referring to the physical distinctions between male and female living things. Sex is merely a manifestation of Gender on a certain plane of the Great Physical Plane—the plane of organic life. The office of Gender is solely that of creating, producing, generating, etc., and its manifestations are visible on every plane of phenomena.

It is not necessary to take up your time with the well known phenomena of the "attraction and repulsion" of the atoms; chemical affinity; the "loves and hates" of the atomic particles; the attraction or cohesion between the molecules of matter. These facts are too well known to need extended comment from us. But, have you ever considered that all of these things are manifestations of the Gender Principle? And more than this, can you not see the reasonableness of the Hermetic Teachings which assert that the very Law of Gravitation—that strange attraction by reason of which all particles and bodies of matter in the universe tend toward each other—is but another manifestation of the Principle of Gender, which operates in the direction of attracting the Masculine to the Feminine energies, and vice versa?

Let us now pass on to a consideration of the operation of the Principle on the Mental Plane.

The idea of Mental Gender may be explained in a few words to students who are familiar with modern psychological theories. The Masculine Principle of Mind corresponds to the so-called Conscious Mind; Objective Mind; Voluntary Mind; Active Mind, etc. And the Feminine Principle of Mind corresponds to the so-called Sub-conscious Mind; Subjective Mind; Involuntary Mind; Passive Mind, etc. Of course the Hermetic Teachings do not agree with the many modern theories regarding the nature of the two phases of mind, nor do they admit many of the facts claimed for the two respective aspects.

The Hermetic Teachers impart their instruction regarding this subject by bidding their students examine the report of their consciousness regarding their Self. The students are bidden to turn their attention inward upon the Self dwelling within each. Each student is led to see that his consciousness gives him first a report of the existence of his Self—the report is "I Am." This at first seems to be the final words from the consciousness, but a little further examination discloses that this "I Am" may be separated or split into two distinct parts, or aspects, which while working in unison and in conjunction, yet, nevertheless, may be separated in consciousness.

While at first there seems to be only an "I" existing, a more careful and closer examination reveals the fact that there exists an "I" and a "Me." These mental twins differ in their characteristics and nature, and an examination of their nature and the phenomena arising from them will throw much light upon many of the problems of mental influence.

Let us begin with a consideration of the "Me," which is usually mistaken for the "I" by the student, until he presses the inquiry a little further back into the recesses of consciousness. A man thinks of his Self (in its aspect of "Me") as being composed of certain feelings, tastes, likes, dislikes, habits, peculiar ties, characteristics, etc., all of which go to make up his personality, or the "Self" known to himself and others. He knows that these emotions and feelings change; are born and die away; are subject to the Principle of Rhythm, and the Principle of Polarity, which take him from one extreme of feeling to another. He also thinks of the "Me" as being certain knowledge gathered together in his mind, and thus forming a part of himself. This is the "Me" of a man.

But we have proceeded too hastily. The "Me" of many men may be said to consist largely of their consciousness of the body and their physical appetites, etc. Their consciousness being largely bound up with their bodily nature, they practically "live there." Some men even go so far as to regard their personal apparel as a part of their "Me," and actually seem to consider it a part of themselves. They cannot conceive of a Self independent of the body. Their mind seems to them to be practically "a something belonging to" their body—which in many cases it is indeed.

But as man rises in the scale of consciousness he is able to disentangle his "Me" from his idea of body, and is able to think of his body as "belonging to" the mental part of him. But even then he is very apt to identify the "Me" entirely with the mental states, feelings, etc., which he feels to exist within him. He is very apt to consider these internal states as identical with himself, instead of their being simply "things" produced by some part of his mentality, and existing within him—of him, and in him, but still not "himself." He sees that he may change these internal states of feelings by an effort of will, and that he may produce a feeling or state of an exactly opposite nature, in the same way, and yet the same "Me" exists. And so after a while he is able to set aside these various mental states, emotions, feelings, habits, qualities, characteristics, and other personal mental belongings—he is able to set them aside in the "not-me" collection of curiosities and encumbrances, as well as valuable possessions. This requires much mental concentration and power of mental analysis on the part of the student. But still the task is possible for the advanced student, and even those not so far advanced are able to see, in the imagination, how the process may be performed.

After this laying-aside process has been performed, the student will find himself in conscious possession of a "Self" which may be considered in its "I" and "Me" dual aspects. The "Me" will be felt to be a Something mental in which thoughts, ideas, emotions, feelings, and other mental states may be produced. It may be considered as the "mental womb," as the ancients styled it—capable of generating mental offspring. It reports to the consciousness as a "Me" with latent powers of creation and generation of mental progeny of all sorts and kinds. Its powers of creative energy are felt to be enormous. But still it seems to be conscious that it must receive some form of energy from either its "I" companion, or else from some other "I," ere it is able to bring into being its mental creations. This consciousness brings with it a realization of an enormous capacity for mental work and creative ability.

But the student soon finds that this is not all that he finds within his inner consciousness. He finds that there exists a mental Something which is able to Will that the "Me" act along certain creative lines, and which is also able to stand aside and witness the mental creation. This part of himself he is taught to call his "I." He is able to rest in its consciousness at will. He finds there not a consciousness of an ability to generate and actively create, in the sense of the gradual process attendant upon mental operations, but rather a sense and consciousness of an ability to project an energy from the "I" to the "Me"—a process of "willing" that the mental creation begin and proceed. He also finds that the "I" is able to stand aside and witness the operations of the "Me's" mental creation and generation. There is this dual aspect in the mind of every person. The "I" represents the Masculine Principle of Mental Gender—the "Me" represents the Female Principle. The "I" represents the Aspect of Being; the "Me" the Aspect of Becoming.

The tendency of the Feminine Principle is always in the direction of receiving impressions, while the tendency of the Masculine Principle is always in the direction of giving out, or expressing. The Feminine Principle has a much more varied field of operation than has the Masculine Principle. The Feminine Principle conducts the work of generating new thoughts, concepts, ideas, including the work of the imagination. The Masculine Principle contents itself with the work of the "Will," in its varied phases. And yet without the active aid of the Will of the Masculine Principle, the Feminine Principle is apt to rest content with generating mental images which are the result of impressions received from outside, instead of producing original mental creations.

Persons who can give continued attention and thought to a subject actively employ both of the Mental Principles—the Feminine in the work of active mental generation, and the Masculine Will in stimulating and energizing the creative portion of the mind. The majority of persons really employ the Masculine Principle but little, and are content to live according to the thoughts and ideas instilled into the "Me" from the "I" of other minds.

The Masculine Principle in the average person is too lazy to act—the display of Will-Power is too slight—and the consequence is that such persons are ruled almost entirely by the minds and wills of other persons. How few original thoughts or original actions are performed by the average person? Are not the majority of persons mere shadows and echoes of others having stronger wills or minds than themselves? The trouble is that the average person dwells almost altogether in his "Me" consciousness, and does not realize that he has such a thing as an "I." He is polarized in his Feminine Principle of Mind, and the Masculine Principle, in which is lodged the Will, is allowed to remain inactive and not employed.

The strong men and women of the world invariably manifest the Masculine Principle of Will, and their strength depends materially upon this fact. Instead of living upon the impressions made upon their minds by others, they dominate their own minds by their Will, obtaining the kind of mental images desired, and moreover dominate the minds of others likewise, in the same manner. Look at the strong people, how they manage to implant their seed-thoughts in the minds of the masses of the people, thus causing the latter to think thoughts in accordance with the desires and wills of the strong individuals. This is why the masses of people are such sheep-like creatures, never originating an idea of their own, nor using their own powers of mental activity.

The manifestation of Mental Gender may be noticed all around us in everyday life. The magnetic persons are those who are able to use the Masculine Principle in the way of impressing their ideas upon others. The actor who makes people weep or cry as he wills, is employing this principle. And so is the successful orator, statesman, preacher, writer or other people who are before the public attention. In this principle lies the secret of personal magnetism, personal influence, fascination, etc., as well as the phenomena generally grouped under the name of Hypnotism.

The student who has familiarized himself with the phenomena generally spoken of as "psychic" will have discovered the important part played in the said phenomena by that force which science has styled "Suggestion," by which term is meant the process or method whereby an idea is transferred to or "impressed upon" the mind of another, causing the second mind to act in accordance. A correct understanding of Suggestion is necessary in order to intelligently comprehend the varied psychical phenomena which Suggestion underlies. But, still more is a knowledge of Vibration and Mental Gender necessary for the student of Suggestion. For the whole principle of Suggestion depends upon the principle of Mental Gender and Vibration.

If you will think of the matter in the light of the Hermetic Teachings, you will be able to see that the energizing of the Feminine Principle by the Vibratory Energy of the Masculine Principle is in accordance to the universal laws of nature. The Hermetic Teachings show that the very creation of the Universe follows the same law, and that in all creative manifestations, upon the planes of the spiritual, the mental, and the physical, there is always in operation this principle of Gender—this manifestation of the Masculine and the Feminine Principles. "As above, so below; as below, so above." And more than this, when the principle of Mental Gender is once grasped and understood, the varied phenomena of psychology at once becomes capable of intelligent classification and study. The principle "works out" in practice, because it is based upon the immutable universal laws of life.

With the aid of The Kybalion one may go through any occult library anew, the old Light from Egypt illuminating many dark pages and obscure subjects. That is the purpose of this book. We do not come expounding a new philosophy, but rather furnishing the outlines of a great world-old teaching, which will make clear the teachings of others—which will serve as a Great Reconciler of differing theories, and opposing doctrines.

Chapter Twelve

Hermetic Axioms

"The possession of Knowledge, unless accompanied by a manifestation and expression in Action, is like the hoarding of precious metals—a vain and foolish thing. Knowledge, like Wealth, is intended for Use. The Law of Use is Universal, and he who violates it suffers by reason of his conflict with natural forces." —The Kybalion.

The Hermetic Teachings, while always having been kept securely locked up in the minds of the fortunate possessors thereof, for reasons that we have already stated, were never intended to be merely stored away and secreted. The Law of Use is dwelt upon in the Teachings, as you may see by reference to the above quotation from The Kybalion, which states it forcibly. Beware of Mental Miserliness, and express into Action that which you have learned. Study the Axioms and Aphorisms, but practice them also.

We give below some of the more important Hermetic Axioms from The Kybalion, with a few comments added to each. Make these your own, and practice and use them, for they are not really your own until you have Used them.

"To change your mood or mental state—change your vibration."—The Kybalion

One may change his mental vibrations by an effort of Will, in the direction of deliberately fixing the Attention upon a more desirable state. Will directs the Attention, and Attention changes the Vibration. Cultivate the Art of Attention, by means of the Will, and you have solved the secret of the Mastery of Moods and Mental States.

"To destroy an undesirable rate of mental vibration, put into operation the Principle of Polarity and concentrate upon the opposite pole to that which you desire to suppress. Kill out the undesirable by changing its polarity."—The Kybalion

This is one of the most important of the Hermetic Formulas. We have shown you that a mental state and its opposite were merely the two poles of one thing, and that by Mental Transmutation the polarity might be reversed. This principle is known to modern psychologists, who apply it to the breaking up of undesirable habits by bidding their students concentrate upon the opposite quality. If you are possessed of Fear, do not waste time trying to "kill out" Fear, but instead cultivate the quality of Courage, and the Fear will disappear. Some writers have expressed this idea most forcibly by using the illustration of the dark room. You do not have to shovel out or sweep out the Darkness, but by merely opening the shutters and letting in the Light the Darkness has disappeared. To kill out a Negative quality, concentrate upon the Positive Pole of that same quality, and the vibrations will gradually change from Negative to Positive, until finally you will become polarized on the Positive pole instead of the Negative. The reverse is also true, as many have found out to their sorrow, when they have allowed themselves to vibrate too constantly on the Negative pole of things. By changing your polarity you may master your moods, change your mental states, remake your disposition, and build up character. Much of the Mental Mastery of the advanced Hermetics is due to this application of Polarity, which is one of the important aspects of Mental Transmutation. Remember the Hermetic Axiom (quoted previously), which says:

"Mind (as well as metals and elements) may be transmuted from state to state; degree to degree; condition to condition; pole to pole; vibration to vibration."—The Kybalion

The mastery of Polarization is the mastery of the fundamental principles of Mental Transmutation or Mental Alchemy, for unless one acquires the art of changing his own polarity, he will be unable to affect his environment. An understanding of this principle will enable one to change his own Polarity, as well as that of others, if he will but devote the time, care, study, and practice necessary to master the art. The principle is true, but the results obtained depend upon the persistent patience and practice of the student.

"Rhythm may be neutralized by an application of the Art of Polarization."—The Kybalion

As we have explained in previous chapters, the Hermetists hold that the Principle of Rhythm manifests on the Mental Plane as well as on the Physical Plane, and that the bewildering succession of moods, feelings, emotions, and other mental states, are due to the backward and forward swing of the mental pendulum, which carries us from one extreme of feeling to the other. The Hermetists also teach that the Law of Neutralization enables one, to a great extent, to overcome the operation of Rhythm in consciousness. As we have explained, there is a Higher Plane of Consciousness, as well as the ordinary Lower Plane, and the

Master by rising mentally to the Higher Plane causes the swing of the mental pendulum to manifest on the Lower Plane, and he, dwelling on his Higher Plane, escapes the consciousness of the swing backward. This is effected by polarizing on the Higher Self, and thus raising the mental vibrations of the Ego above those of the ordinary plane of consciousness. It is akin to rising above a thing, and allowing it to pass beneath you. The advanced Hermetist polarizes himself at the Positive Pole of his Being—the "I Am" pole rather than the pole of personality, and by "refusing" and "denying" the operation of Rhythm, raises himself above its plane of consciousness, and standing firm in his Statement of Being he allows the pendulum to swing back on the Lower Plane without changing his Polarity. This is accomplished by all individuals who have attained any degree of self-mastery, whether they understand the law or not. Such persons simply "refuse" to allow themselves to be swung back by the pendulum of mood and emotion, and by steadfastly affirming the superiority, they remain polarized on the Positive pole. The Master, of course, attains a far greater degree of proficiency, because he understands the law which he is overcoming by a higher law, and by the use of his Will he attains a degree of Poise and Mental Steadfastness almost impossible of belief on the part of those who allow themselves to be swung backward and forward by the mental pendulum of moods and feelings.

Remember, always, however, that you do not really destroy the Principle of Rhythm, for that is indestructible. You simply overcome one law by counter-balancing it with another, and thus maintain an equilibrium.

"Nothing escapes the Principle of Cause and Effect, but there are many Planes of Causation, and one may use the laws of the higher to overcome the laws of the lower."—The Kybalion

By an understanding of the practice of Polarization, the Hermetists rise to a higher plane of Causation and thus counter-balance the laws of the lower planes of Causation. By rising above the plane of ordinary Causes they become themselves, in a degree, Causes instead of being merely Caused. By being able to master their own moods and feelings, and by being able to neutralize Rhythm, as we have already explained, they are able to escape a great part of the operations of Cause and Effect on the ordinary plane. The masses of people are carried along, obedient to their environment; the wills and desires of others stronger than themselves; the effects of inherited tendencies; the suggestions of those about them; and other outward causes; which tend to move them about on the chessboard of life like mere pawns. By rising above these influencing causes, the advanced Hermetists seek a higher plane of mental action, and by dominating their moods, emotions, impulses, and feelings, they create for themselves new characters, qualities, and powers, by which they overcome their ordinary environment. Such people help to play the game of life understandingly, instead of being moved about this way and that way by stronger influences and powers and wills. As The Kybalion says:

"The wise ones serve on the higher, but rule on the lower. They obey the laws coming from above them, but on their own plane, and those below them, they rule and give orders. And, yet, in so doing, they form a part of the Principle, instead of opposing it. The wise man falls in with the Law, and by understanding its movements he operates it instead of being its blind slave. Just as does the skilled swimmer turn this way and that way, going and coming as he will, instead of being as the log which is carried here and there—so is the wise man as compared to the ordinary man—and yet both swimmer and log, wise man and fool, are subject to Law. He who understands this is well on the road to Mastery."

In conclusion let us again call your attention to the Hermetic Axiom: "True Hermetic Transmutation is a Mental Art."—The Kybalion

In the above axiom, the Hermetists teach that the great work of influencing one's environment is accomplished by Mental Power. The Universe being wholly mental, it follows that it may be ruled only by Mentality. Back of and under the teachings of the various cults and schools, remains ever constant the principle of the Mental Substance of the Universe. If the Universe be Mental in its substantial nature, then it follows that Mental Transmutation must change the conditions and phenomena of the Universe. If the Universe is Mental, then Mind must be the highest power affecting its phenomena. If this be understood then all the so-called "miracles" and "wonder-workings" are seen plainly for what they are.

"THE ALL is MIND; The Universe is Mental."
—The Kybalion

"Three Initiates" is one of several pseudonyms used by WILLIAM WALKER ATKINSON, a popular and innovative New Thought writer and publisher in the early twentieth century. Born in Baltimore, Maryland, in 1862, Atkinson became a successful attorney in 1894. Following a series of illnesses, he immersed himself in New Thought literature. He soon became an important figure in the early days of the movement, publishing magazines such as *Suggestion, New Thought*, and *Advanced Thought*. Under the aegis of his own publishing company, Yogi Publication Society, Atkinson authored many bylined works and many titles written under the pseudonyms Yogi Ramacharaka, Magus Incognito, and Theron Q. Dumont. *The Kybalion* is the most popular and enduring work published by Atkinson's Chicago-based publishing house, and is perhaps the most widely read occult work of the twentieth century. Atkinson died in California in 1932.

MITCH HOROWITZ, who abridged and introduced this volume, is the PEN Award-winning author of books including *Occult America* and *The Miracle Club: How Thoughts Become Reality.* *The Washington Post* says Mitch "treats esoteric ideas and movements with an even-handed intellectual studiousness that is too often lost in today's raised-voice discussions." Follow him @MitchHorowitz.